Cutting the Clouds Towards

Other books by Matt Simpson

Making Arrangements
(Bloodaxe 1982)

An Elegy for the Galosherman –
New & Selected Poems
(Bloodaxe 1990)

Catching Up with History
(Bloodaxe 1995)

For children

The Pigs' Thermal Underwear
(Headland 1994)

Matt, Wes and Pete
(Macmillan 1995)
reissued in 1998
as *Lost Property Box*

Cutting the Clouds Towards

MATT SIMPSON

LIVERPOOL UNIVERSITY PRESS

First published 1998 by
LIVERPOOL UNIVERSITY PRESS
Liverpool L69 3BX

British Library Cataloguing-in-Publication Data
A British Library CIP record is available

ISBN 0–85323–713–1

Design and production: Janet Allan

Typeset in 12/14 pt Bodoni
by Wilmaset Ltd, Birkenhead, Wirral
Printed by Print in Black, Midsomer Norton, Bath

ACKNOWLEDGEMENTS
The poem contained in the section *To Tasmania with Mrs Meredith*
were first published by Headland Press in 1994; those in *On the
Right Side of the Earth* (with the exception of *Threads, Journal
Entry for Tuesday, 31st Oct.* and *Making an Exhibition*) were
published by Queen Victoria Museum & Art Gallery, Launceston,
Tasmania in 1995. Individual poems have appeared in *The Argotist,
Brando's Hat, Contact, Drumbeat* (Australia), *Poetry Wales, Prop,
Writing from Tasmania* edited by C. A. Cranston; and some have
appeared in *Making Connections – a festschrift for Matt Simpson*
edited by Angela Topping, Stride Publications, 1996. Extract from
Collected Poems 1909–1939 by William Carlos Williams reprinted
by permission of Carcanet Press.
    Photographs by courtesy of Allport Library and Museum of
Fine Arts, State Library of Tasmania.

Contents

Preface

The poems collected here were the product – before, during and after – of a two-month residency in Tasmania in the Autumn of 1995. The residency was hosted by the Queen Victoria Museum & Art Gallery, Launceston, and coincided in its first week with the Tasmanian Poetry Festival. It was supported by Cornford Press and the British Council.

Most of the poems are responses to encounters with the work and life of the mid-nineteenth-century writer and artist, Louisa Anne Meredith, who spent the first part of her life in Birmingham and who was already established as author and artist before, at the age of twenty-seven, she married her cousin, Charles, and sailed for Australia in 1839.

The Headland booklet was dedicated to Dimitris Tsaloumas and the Queen Victoria Museum publication to Kaye Dowling and Tim Thorne.

The present collection is dedicated to the many people who were kind and generous to me during the residency.

Matt Simpson,
Liverpool, 1995

Foreword by John Lucas

It's not what we do with facts that matters, Robert Frost said, it's what the facts do with us. Fact: Matt Simpson was born in Liverpool to a Merchant Navy father whose roll-call of exotic places where ships had taken him included Tasmania's capital, Hobart. 'When he mentioned Hobart', the poet says, 'there was always a twinkle in my father's eye that suggested some kind of romantic experience.' Fact: Matt Simpson was from September to November, 1995, poet-in-residence at the Queen Victoria Museum and Art Gallery in Launceston, Tasmania. Before he left England he had come across and read *My Home in Tasmania*, the journal of the writer and artist, Louisa Anne Meredith. Meredith, whose maiden name was Twamley, had been born in Birmingham in 1812, from where she emigrated to Australia newly-married to her cousin, Charles Meredith, in 1839. After a year in New South Wales they made a nightmarish ten-day voyage from Sydney to Hobart with their three-month first born, Charles. For the best part of the next forty years, which contained more than a fair share of hardship and during which they raised three sons (one died in infancy), they lived in various parts of Tasmania but mostly along its north east coast. After Charles' death in Launceston in 1879 his widow moved to a flat in Hobart and, then, in 1895, transferred to Melbourne, where she died a few months later.

So much for the facts. What they did to Matt Simpson is evident from the following pages. The poems we now have are made up from two pamphlet-length collections. The first, a fourteen-poem sequence entitled *To Tasmania with Mrs Meredith: Explorations*, was published by Headland Press in 1994, after the poet had encountered *My Home in Tasmania* but before he arrived on the island itself. The second, *On the Right Side of the Earth*, was published by the Queen Victoria Museum and Art Gallery in Launceston to coincide with Matt Simpson's final presentation of his work as poet-in-residence. The presentation took place on Friday 12th November, 1995, just two weeks after the centenary of Louisa Anne Meredith's death. In the weeks prior to this Simpson had written no fewer than twenty-three poems exploring in different ways his sense of engagement with a person, a place, and, more remarkably, of hers and its with him. For among the most astonishing features of this intensely creative engagement is the way Mrs Meredith herself emerges as a full and complex character, witty, resilient, keenly observant, even able to rebuke the poet for his 'arrogance of hindsight'. And there is also, more elusive, but strongly felt for all that, the poet's Liverpudlian father, his presence – to use a Yeatsian term – intuited in Hobart, where the poet, in town to give a reading of his own work at the Bavarian Tavern (in Liverpool Street!) sees 'a me / some ten years on'. Yet with scrupulous tact he admits that such a meeting in that southernmost port, 'almost what I had come for', is, as the poem's necessarily ambiguous title informs us, 'About As Far As We Can Go'.

But if this suggests a possible thwarting, the sequence as a whole testifies to that melding process out of which true art is made. This includes the gathering in of one further fact, as it can properly be called. Matt Simpson is throughout aware of, may be said almost to be haunted by, another island discovered, another father lost and transformed, other voices set free. It takes a rare poet to risk weaving into his own work moments from and allusions to *The Tempest*, that most authoritative if mysterious of plays, but the following poems triumphantly surmount that danger. That they should do so helps us to recognise how assured and compelling is Matt Simpson's achievement.

Prologue

For I
Have given you a thread of mine own life.

Ship in a Bottle

Below the kirk, below the hill,
Below the lighthouse top.

I'd promised others and myself
that I would leave it all behind,
this quizzing mirrors
for his face.

Now here's
this hark-back thing
he made at sea
my stepmother kept and I
have coveted for years.

'Take it,' she says
too casually.

*

Making this, he too
was harking back
to how his father knew the sea,
massive rollings under men.

It's his equivalent of poem.

*

He means it for *The Cutty Sark:*
sleek black hull, rigging taut
with readiness, bowsprit raring to go,
gulls silent at the turn of tide,
houses, church, and lighthouse,
faces steadfast with goodbyes,
and then that first swell
felt in the muscle lifting the deck.

*

If I am to go anywhere with this
I must believe in voyages
and mainly in my own:
the Tasmania he set foot in
half-a-century ago, where
he knocked-'em-back
along the Hobart waterfront.

Ships like this (I mean
the ones that hauled
the convicts out) were eight
months roughing it.

He would ride it taking two.

I get whisked there in a day.

*

It speaks of silence,
infinite poising of the tide;
waves of putty never meant to lift.

Like Keats's little town, streets
are desolate; captain, bosun have
no cheering shouts to raise;

the ship's forever doldrum'd
on a painted sea.

*

If I dragged its stopper out,
or if by accident I smashed the glass

it would release a soundless sigh
like his that afternoon I watched him die.

To Tasmania with Mrs Meredith

*I think he will carry this island home in his
pocket and give it his son for an apple.*

At Sea with Mrs Meredith

Ten days at sea from Sydney down a coast
of bays and rocks (all which she sketched) to Hobarton;

squalls to brave, in as rotten carcass of a tub
as ever sullied Neptune's blue. Half-dreamy and half-dead,

(that slide-door to-and-fro-ing like a pendulum!)
she smiled at the miseries of heroines in books

a friend of Mr Meredith supplied for her;
then dirty water dripping on the bed; and once

a fork-tailed centipede fell on her cap
scarpering with railroad rapidity, more venomous,

she knew, than any scorpion's sting. Thank God
the dangerous reptile landed where it did,

not on the baby's head! The sooty beams in any case
were cluttered with woodlice; the ship

a leaking brewer's vat, half-rigged, in want
of top-gallants, studding sails: all which she braved

to gain a temperate clime, a life of health and strength
where the fair promise of infancy might have

prospect of being realised. Remembering
a nervous hubbub of voices, footsteps clattering, then

vehement flappings of a sail blown from its ropes,
another thunderously buffeted, rigging twanging, blocks

thudding about in aptly-named Storm Bay, cliffs sheer
to leeward, weather thick, squally, never-ending rain.

At length they dropped anchor where jingling chains
proved choicer music than any concerto she had ever heard.

What Mr Meredith asked the Ship's Owner about Dick

Dick here, Dick there, Dick everywhere!

If ever ubiquity fell to the lot of mortal . . .

Dick!   *take Mr Jones some hot water*
          Mr Jones wants his coat brushed
          bring a light in the cabin
          go and swab the deck
          peel then 'taturs for cook
          you scoundrel, steward says
          you've not cleaned his knives

Dick!   *go and water the sheep*
          help reef the topsails
          feed the geese
          take these bones to the dog

Smart active lad,
some ten or twelve years old?
seems to execute
your multifarious orders, sir,
with the most unflinching alacrity,

I take it an apprentice, sir?

No,   *he ain't a'prentice,*
       he's a nevy of mine
       as come aboard
       for a holiday!

Mrs Meredith looks about her

So like an English Spring,
a showery Midlands May! Except
it's Autumn. Nonetheless

in little gardens of snug
Tasmanian houses, great bushes
of geraniums sprout

like stout and rosy children.
And there are mulberries,
such spectacle of *reds*,

cherries, currants, strawberries,
of *greens*, gooseberries, apples,
swollen pears. Veritable confectionery

of quinces, medlars,
plums! Preserver's paradise,
pickler's dream. And, O,

abundances of peaches,
such plump babies' tender skins!
The forests promise walnuts,

clustering filberts. Here
vines succeed and, although
often nipped at night by frost,

even potatoes dream of Home.

Mrs Meredith and Hobart Culture

Such small-town-mindedness! Sir John
and Lady Franklin spared no pains
to rouse a taste for science, literature and art.

Her soirées in the *conversazione* style
were never popular. A very general *one-ness*
prevailed as to the fad for dancing

among pretty Tasmanians with no feeling for
rooms crammed with pictures, books,
shells, stone – dust-gatherers! Nothing

to do but hear people talk lectures,
else sit mute as mice and listen to
what's called Good Music. Why, they moaned,

couldn't she engage a military band,
roll up the carpets and, instead of all
that scientific, philosophic guff, just *dance?*

Mrs Meredith and Hunting

A scratch pack of two
or three couple hounds
driving a tame imported deer
to the very verge of existence,
then, would you believe,
rescuing it for further chase!

Even a kangaroo they'll tally-ho
with all the show and pretence
of sanctified pursuit,

all underwritten by noble
and Christian worthies,
these exploits of the field
are turned into
grandiloquent narratives
by so-called correspondents

who deem it sport
to see some poor tame stag –
as was the case
a week before we came –
antlers snarling in a tree,
gralloched, dead.

Flora and Fossil

*   Above Hobart

Great numbers of singular 'grass trees'
(*Xanthorrea arborea*), all ages and growths,
short, tall, straight, and crooked,
each with a long tressed head of rushy leaves.

*   On the Road from Jerusalem

Straggling dingy gum trees (*Eucalyptus*),
wattle and honeysuckle-trees (*Acacia*
and *Banksia*) and 'cutting grass' so sharp
dogs have been injured running there.

Delighted to see some fern
like common forest-fern or brake back home,
but stunted, crisped with drought.

*   At Richmond

The then police magistrate, geologist and virtuoso,
                    afforded us
an agreeable evening. Many limestone fossils
                    were new to me.
The room in which my poor maid slept was stored
                    with choice and bulky
specimens, such *skillintons and dead men's bones*
                    as bad
as vaultses under churches, death's heads, cross-bones
                    she went
and had *such horrid odorous dreams.*

Mrs Meredith goes a-Gypsying
and enjoys a Barbecue

Let me expound the mystery
of 'sticker-up' cookery.
First slice your kangaroo
cutlets, three or two
inch broad, one third thick.
Next cut a stick
that's four feet long,
making sure it's clean and strong.
Spit your cutlets on —
which end? — the narrower one!

Now here's the trick! Thread
upon its sharpened head
some delicately rosy bacon.
Thrust your stake in
to leeward of the fire.
Soon will start a choir
of frizzle, splutter, steam.
Just you see the bacon gleam!
As the bacon softens, watch
a lubricating shower of rich
and savoury tears downflow
to the leaner kangaroo below.

'And gentlemen,' as gay
old Mr Hardcastle would say
if he were dining in the great outdoor
'there is really nothing more
enticing to a hungry man at least
than being in attendance at this kind of feast.
There are times I feel my poor heart breaking
for stuck-up kangaroo and bacon!'

Though to be fair,
kangaroo's a lot like hare.

The Merediths attend a Ceremony

The Government Gardens here
may not be quite so gorgeous as the ones
in Sydney, not as rich in glowing oranges,
scarlet pomegranates, golden loquats,
but, well, they *are* more homely and, to use
my favourite and much-travelled term of praise,
so *English*-looking: roses, roses everywhere
and pleasant drives among groves
of native trees. Naturally, we
were present at the ceremony, the laying of
the first stone of the new Government House
overlooking the Derwent. The Lieutenant
Governor and his cultivated wife arranged
a collation in the charming rustic lodge;
and when the band struck up there were at once
quadrilles upon the lawn – although
to be honest, rather in the dust, since there
the turf was something of the scantiest.

Mrs Meredith speaks of the Good
Old Days of Privatisation . . .

The minute that they landed us
Upon that dreadful shore,
The planters they inspected us,
Full twenty score and more.
They led us round like horses
And sold us out of hand
And yoked us to the plough my boys
To plough Van Diemen's Land.

. . . when idle, unprincipled outcasts
were *assignable*, once set ashore,
to private service: ploughmen,
shepherds, shearers, reapers,
butchers, gardeners, masons,
shoe-makers, house-servants,

being persons of like class,

required to separate
from their former partners in crime
as the first great step
toward reformation,

huts to live in, doubtless more
commodious than the ones they left
back home, with as much fuel
as they chose to cut themselves,
abundant rations of food, allowances
of clothing, bedding, boots,

and the chance to show
their latent goodness, slough off
notorious idleness, become industrious,
trustworthy servants, earn
tickets-of-leave so they might

hire themselves elsewhere
for wages. So manifest
are this system's advantages that settlers
prefer ticket-of-leave men,

who, sentence served,
gain conditional pardon,
free range of all
the Australian colonies. Some achieve
free pardons in the end!

How could anyone utter such words
as 'white slavery' or
other opprobrious epithets?
You see how progressive, how
proven the system was!

So when in that perfidious year
of '42, they changed *assignment*
to *probation*, made
hard-labour gangs do public works,
the good was all undone:

man naturally willing and diligent
lapsed into apathetic drones.

You Rambling Boys of Liverpool

Oh, Dirty Maggie May,
They have taken you away . . .
You robbed full many a sailor
Also a couple of whalers
And now you're doing time in Bot'ny Bay.

And not just Maggie Mays never to walk
down Lime Street anymore, but you rambling boys
with your dog, your gun, your snare.

Let's sing it for Jimmy Murphy, Paddy Malone,
the likes of me, poachers, trespassers all,
Mary Johnson too who took the captain's fancy

so's he married her off-hand, hauled out
of salty Liverpool for a-chasing of the game.
Here's a curse on keepers, with their oiled

shot guns and hounds, damn their singular lugholes,
the periwigged beak with his mallet and posh words,
and a curse on this vessel for creaking and tumbling

on the raging sea, the ocean wide – all
for the snap of a rabbit's neck, the squeak
of a pheasant, the rustle of dew-dank fern.

As I lay in the hold one night
A-dreaming all alone
I dreamt I was in Liverpool,
Way back in my old home
With my true love beside me
And a jug of ale in hand,
When I woke quite broken-hearted
Lying off Van Diemen's Land.

The Call of the Genes

And you, dad, with rusty cut-water
hauling out of Liverpool
inside a riveted bucket of a thing,

what tickled your fancy down-under there
in the Roaring Forties?
What apple blossom made your bosun's eye

twinkle thinking of Hobart? Who was
the girl-in-port you hoarded like pay slips?
Are there any more not home like me?

Dear Mrs Meredith

Saying I admire your work may sound
a corny way of opening but it doesn't mean
it isn't true. In any case
I know it's something writers like to hear.

I envy your fortitude, doughtiness that comes
with the philosophy that Life's a trial,
World a testing place, taking it on the chin —
that chancy voyage for a start,
main and mizzen top masts down. Then

there's your rascally (I mean it politely)
good humour, that bit about the centipede
scuttling off *with a railroad rapidity*,
the common bush track which wet weather beat
to a *tenacious batter-pudding consistency*;
not to mention your downright curiosity,
water-colourist concern with how things look;

and wanting to be liberal, to believe
in Progress or in the thing called Good
which *ignorance and idleness alone impede*;
not least your (I think that I can safely say)
woman's way of dealing with the world . . .

Going about like Adam, though,
conferring names on flora, fauna, settlements,
I'm not so sure you understood as colonising,
locating power, legitimising sovereignty, even if
you were generous enough to think the more
euphonious native names, *Wollondilly*, *Wollongong*,
Wooloomooloo, *Illawarra*, *Maneroo*, preferable
to English ones with their unfair comparisons
between the great and old, the little and the new.

Some things you were blind to. They went
halloo-ing after Abos, those horseback gentlemen
and wielding of the cat was far *more* liberal,
dear Mrs M, than you could be. Just think,
those convicts' leg-irons *half* your comfortable weight!
Doubtless you knew but had your loyalties to weigh?

Dear Mr Simpson

At times we teeter on the brink,
seeing before us all we wish to have
and be, the stasis (where the poems are)
between the promise and the act.

On the Right Side of the Earth

For he is sure i' th' island

Louisa Anne Meredith (née Twamley) in middle age.

We meet at last

This is what
you look like then?

An obvious
charmer still,

hand on shoulder
fingering curls.

We meet at Warrandyte,
the good professor's house

where distant bell birds ping
and magpies chortle in

the pepper trees.
I mean I get to see

a frontispiece. The *carte
de visite* photographer

has gone for that soft-focus
pre-Raphaelite look

the men all like:
that studied ambivalence,

noli me tangere yet
console me in my hour of need.

I know – for I have miles
of retrospect –

that your if-only eyes
are artist's eyes,

the company you yearn for
is angels different from

the ones aloft: you want
luminaries of the brush and pen.

And there are fraught times ahead,
counting the lost, the dead,

the Swan River flood,
terror-stricken horses straining necks,

and only just,
above the battering water line.

I've been wanting to ask . . .

Stuffed parrots and wild flowers
from Van Diemen's Land, four months
down holds of scudding ships,
which cousins, remember, sent and you
put under glass in your very own
painting room, where you, just like
your easel, were set up, with not
the least idea of venturings – that ear
drum of a whale from *dear, dear Charles*
on the chimney piece with purpose only
to confound, provide after-dinner jousts
of wit.
      Engravings, your own paintings
up on the walls, bookcases smug
with well-heeled tomes, a crisp drawer
of shells, stern busts, *your* china, and even
the pelt of a thylacine. You had it made,
Louisa Anne, *artist, scribbler*, at home
among your curiosities, the Midlands great
outdoors all yours to go a-sketching in –
luxuriating, your word. One
disappointment, though: the nautilus shell
that didn't come, *dear Uncle George!*
who then, *insensitive!* invited you Down Under,
as governess to his brood!
      Where would be
my literature? Sonnets to whales and porpoises!
Canzonets to kangaroos, madrigals to merinos!
Dirges to black swans!
      And, oh dear, Mrs M,
did you say *portraits of engaging*
lovely natives there?

(Remember *This island's mine which thou tak'st from me*).

        Were you on the rebound then?
Was it terror of the shelf? Was it love
made you, against your mother's wish
(seventy years and in poor health), abandon Brum,
set out with the chap who'd parcelled up
that extraordinary bit of whale?

Dear Mr Simpson

You got here safely then?
And, my word, in a day! Ensconsed
in a gatekeeper's cottage at the Gorge.

Do you find it comfortable? What about
the fogs? The possums clumping
in the rafters and, as you say, that

pesky little paddle boat? I understand
someone has written a book about me? Well!
A bit late now, unless you've faith

in that old hag Posterity,
but not much good if you feel your life's
been all askew. Go on then,

publish your poems about me
if it makes you feel any better. But remember,
if there's applause, who got here first.

Taking things in

You were extending language
to take things in,

driven by curiosity,
the collector's fetish
thoroughness, the thrill
of discovering novelty.

You came to describe.

To whom? A foreign language
is a thief. Translation is
invading imperial instrument . . .

                                   You
taught me language and my profit on't
Is, I know how to curse.

Not just words
but all your pictures too.

A Bummer

Only in Oz is Elgar called
a *bloke!* G'day, Sir Ed!
I'm tuned in to bright-
n-breezy *Classic FM*

in Launceston – a *Specialist*,
says the visa, an *amiable
grey-bearded British poet*,
says the Press.

Below, the brown river
is sneaking in again,
repainting the crags of Cataract Gorge,
a dumpy tourist paddle-boat

like something off a roundabout,
is gaudily chugging past,
its p.a. barking *There
above you to your right . . .*

*

Launceston wasn't fun for you
in those willow-pattern days,
trundling in in that knocked-up carriage
with your old servant Godbold

decked out in his suit of velveteen,
tall black shiny hat, shot belt, gun.
And what a fog! You imagined a huge
cauldron of steam. And, as always,

perky with opinion,
you ventured the siting of the town
an *unaccountable blunder*. Despite masts
tangling prettily above the wharf,

handsome church at every turn,
river and well-stored shops,
you winced at the squalor, filth,
as if sensing the end of flitting
might insist on this. Clutching faith
in the sunnier side of things,
you left in a pelting thunderstorm.

Swanport

had been a drag:

father-in-law (stickler
by the sound and look of him)
made allowances, thinking you
doubtless *in dread*
of the touch of scarlet fever
on the children but then
asserted *such illusion
dispelled* by your subsequent
avoidance of the place.

And to be sure you believed
it grew yearly more and more
sluggish, monotonous; did not
show yourself the *model
daughter-in-law.*

There was that in you
which would not compromise.
What says that character in Ibsen?
Compromise is the very devil.

But you hated whiskery Henrik
or anything commonplace.
Repulsive, uninteresting
was your typical beef
about his characters and plots.
You sat on your cold-arse monument
impervious to the fact his Nora
in *A Doll's House* smacked of you.

And for the Record

You're not entirely right. *You do yet taste*
Some subtleties o' th' isle that will not let you
Believe things certain. We did enjoy
Launceston. I was tickled pink to see
so much activity. A veritable hive!
You must remember we were five
years in the bush and lacking novelty. To behold
so many new people, horses, vehicles,
neat suburban cottages with coach-houses,
floral gardens, smart green gates,
carts piled high with wood, errand carts jogging,
wagons of people on the move like us
with all their tottering furniture, gigs, phaetons,
pony chaises, folk in spruce dresses,
horses, hounds, for tomorrow's hunt
in Campbell Town. But yes, I *was* critical
of the place, and did not know then
that there my poor dear Charles would die.

Fax from Launceston to Michael

He's at it again, the wise guy
on *ABC Classic FM*: an Overture
of Veracini's is music played
'at the point of a sword';
he just loves it 'when Schumann
lets his horns out to graze.'

Now he wants to put some
'steroids' into the broadcast
with Rachmaninov's Second
Symphony.

*

      You'd be at home
with such irreverence.

          Grainger's
Molly on the Shore 'sounds like
she's driving towards a village
in a tank'; Schubert's Ninth
is 'the Big One, *that'll* take up
the lunch hour!' And, wait for it,
'this is J. S. Bach placing
your wake-up call' with *Wachet Auf*.

*

There are things I'm trying not to miss.

It's one of the raining days . . .
cars more urgent on King's Bridge,
as if home's the best place now.

The South Esk River's lost its sheen . . .
except there, in the shelter of the arch,
one perfect stroke of gloss.

A Hasty Rejoinder

I'm not recolonising, Mrs M, nor here
to put my words into your — nor
into the Island's — mouth,

nor to feel comfortable. I've seen
what's left of Port Arthur, have heard
the guide's hard hellhole narratives,

enough to make me feel
the sometime emptiness of love
and hatreds used to compensate.

Out in the blue harbour
the Isle of the Dead is always going to send
its ghostly stench inland.

I'm obliged of course to underwrite
the wonders of the place;
it's expected and it's right:

cliffs, crags, different-coloured birds,
landscape that's familiar-but-not-quite,
that makes me feel I've Star-Trek'd here,

will suddenly come to
in a staring seminar in Liverpool, babbling
of blue remembered hills and settlements

right out of *Shane*. In a one-horse store
a woman said 'Everywhere you look's
a view.' But views are history too.

Something you can't deny

At Dead Cow Creek the front horse sloshed
into deep black mud. The children
had to be carried. You went downstream
and jumped your mount across. That afternoon,
startled by echoing screams, you wheeled
to find the children's nurse distraught,
blood spouting from the baby's neck. *A leech,
only a leech*, said Charles. And then
Sydney Bill arrived to guide you on
the last long leg. Even so, in gloom
with your poor sight, you kept losing the track.
Ten hours' horseback had you cramped
and chilled to the marrow, hardly aware
of reins or hands, feeling at any time
you might just topple off. Only when you heard
far-off dogs and out of the dark a building loomed,
did you know you had arrived at *Castle Dismal*,
the worst of all your homes-from-home.

Charles Meredith, Louisa's husband, aged fifty-five.

The Interview

So why bring all that up,
our terrible come-down
in the world? All
fiddle-faddle, ungenteel!

> *Times have changed, We don't have*
> *as much faith in aspiration as you;*
> *we want the struggle in the muck*
> *that shows the Human Entity.*

Port Sorell is best forgotten:
I don't want blather about fortitude,
even less about losing
my what, my downcast way!

> *Charles's fault! He had no form*
> *with money, he overspent*
> *building Springvale, was lucky*
> *to be made Police Magistrate.*

Charles was a good man.
You've read the Elegy I penned:
'staunch comrades, true lovers,
side by side through sorrow, joy'?

> *A dab hand at failure; without you*
> *and your pretensions where would he*
> *have got? Those parliamentary bills*
> *were your brainchildren.*

That was later when we were Somebody.
Even my biographer talks
of Triumphant Years! Go to Triabunna,
listen to the bell. And when

you hear it, think kindly of my dear
lamented dead. And let it toll
for one hour at noon on the day
of my burial, whenever that may be.

As for the arrogance
of hindsight, Mr Simpson . . .

In Mount Field National Park

for Jack & Christine Lomax

And we were in
the intimate silence of
the rain forest

and I was listening
with I thought
a deep kind of listening

as if I'd hear
by being still
the Wilderness itself

Eucalyptus Regnans
hurling themselves
upwards through centuries . . .

a sudden bedlam
of whirling parrots screaming . . .

then

News of a Death

> *'Tis far off,*
> *And rather like a dream than an assurance.*

It's odd, love, sleeping in strange beds
twelve thousand miles apart: me Tasmania,
the Artist's Cottage in the Gorge,
where possums scratch the weatherboard,
wake me up at two a.m.; and you
your mother's Berlin flat, the stale smell
of her old habits as what's now left
of her. You phoned tonight
and it wasn't Liverpool but Somewhere Else.

And it's a *Star-Trek* planet I am talking from.
Yesterday a man plonked an *A-to-Z*
of where we live down on the table
after a meal, to make me feel at home,
of roasters, lamb, mint sauce.
I had to show the Bootle I was born in,
the Halewood we live in now. Looking down
from Outer Space, *There*, I said,
my wife's this moment walking the dog.

On the Answering Machine

I heard about your loss and am sorry for it,
even if the Berlin woman was past hope:
a life of acetic sourness obdurately borne.

I think your grandmother was the same,
using grievance to demand respect, blind
to the irony it doesn't come that way
or is not worth having if it does,

so that (your Blake knew this) the *wrath
doth grow*. But you understand that.
And I am conscious I'm not serving you
except with platitudes: death always stings
and your dear wife will be awash with guilt
as daughters will at times like this. It happens.

I'm flattered of course that you're
not flying off (hard for you either way),
and that we will continue our conversations.

I wasn't going to tell you this,
but I'm beginning to have a sneaking regard . . .

In Flowerdale

I have no ambition
to see a goodlier man.

Barney snaps a blade of grass and pokes at a hole
in the old eucalypt up near the house. *Closer*, he tells me,
and, like tuning ancient radios, there's a funny sort of buzz,
sugar gliders trickled pink by his cat's whisker.

In the old landrover he will *not* sell his neighbour for parts
a family of pardalotes is nesting, chicks chuckling
in the wispy chassis . . . and there! like a leaf swooping
(*Did you see him?*) an adult bird too quick for me.

Buddy, buddy! he calls, sprinkling maggots of cheese,
and shiny-in-blue-sequin wrens come hop-skip-and-jump
like he's an Oz St Francis. He takes me this morning
into the Bush, a place of the spirit. It's a kind of initiation,
there's privilege to it, the steep descent into Quartz Creek
down to a green tribe of man ferns it belongs to,
then steeply out again to an immensity of sky.

He tells me stories of black fish, of duke witty's chirrupings,
Hank and Loch his brothers in the warm-sitting-around-comfy
feel of seventy years ago in Flowerdale when Kay his Dad
smoked a sagacious pipe and Mum translated Greek.

Where's morning gone? he asks, then quickly says *Or has it?*
wishing and making me memories too. For it seems the man
tolerates only love round here. There are good sons
in the paddocks with the sturdy cattle . . . but I also see
a dead cow's hooves poking the hugeness of the Flowerdale sky
and there, against a fence, aborted calves with eyes that say
we had our chance in this Edenic Flowerdale but just
missed out. I listen to his quiet talk of being buried here
beneath the silver birch he planted and there's

an OK-ness to it. So Barney here's to you,
it's been a privilege, an honour and a joy. As we in Liverpool
most *definitely* say, god bless ye owld gums is gold!

Hadn't we the Gaiety?

Tell me, laid-back Mary, just what the set-up is,
I need you to be telling me my part in all of this!
All depends, drawls Mary, *you can never guarantee,*
Things sort of happen, just sit back and see.
Laconic laid-back Mary is driving me to Liffey,
A strange bugger from England, sinuses all sniffy.

We hurl the van at Liffey through a streaky-bacon sky,
At jet-black mountains, Mary Szmekura and I,
Till an old weatherboard schoolhouse somehow just appears,
Old Laid-back slamming down through all the growly gears,
And it's open door and a beeline to a cracking log fire
Where someone with a fiddle is bowing higher, higher.

A bit of a squeaky squeezebox, a brace of lithe guitars
Are doling out a strathspey beneath huge Liffey stars;
Then old Mike finds another tune, so it's chocks away
Swerving off to Ireland, hot-foot to Galway Bay.
The playing ends in smiles, shoulders slump and sigh,
Waiting for someone else to start, when suddenly this guy

Quoits his voice into the middle, a Geordie miners' song
Of men weighed down by rockface and bosses who were wrong.
Then someone says *a poem!* and it seems a simple thing
To add my voice to the company as much as those that sing
To an intensity of listening as belonged to long ago
When Pa read out of Scripture, was reverenced doing so.

A fiddle starts a-twiddling, accordians gust in,
A tin whistle's toot-fluting over them, they begin
A jaunty reel that rattles around the walls,
Feet are thumping floorboards; next someone drawls
A gutsy song of billabongs, then I add more poems.
One final jig then maybe? before we head for homes.

But there's a whisper, *Kelly!* who's shut his eyes to play
And is like to start an old lament to snatch the breath away
With a thing that is as soulful as when God himself is sad.
Instinct knew its moment and instinct Kelly had
For the old ache of love and loss and ancient desperate times
Alive and deep in everyone. For him these rhymes.

About as far as we can go

Right then, dad, I have at last
set foot in Hobart,
strolled Salamanca Place.

You'd have
a proper cob on, seeing just
how swish it has become, so
Left Bank, arty-farty shops
and small cafés, young cappuccino'd
long-haireds planning how
to rescue rain forests. No
Ma Dwyer and her *Blue House*.

The Museum at Battery Point
displayed a photograph of a ship
you sailed, a tin-pot of a tub,
black-smoke funnel, straight-up prow.

At *The Bavarian Tavern* I read poems
about you. In a corner sat a *me*
some ten years on . . . beard, glasses
and the nose . . . except his name was Otto,
accent thick with flavours of a kind
– but who can tell? – impossible to us.

It was a moment, almost what
I'd come for, which was to meet
and greet the you-in-me, bosun,
in Salamanca Place.

Your art Mrs Meredith

was one long act
of praise

a bit like
my telling students
to allow themselves
astonishments

and then
articulate them

yes I know
about Buddha's
Flower Sermon
and haiku only needing
the recognition of a smile

I know too
William Carlos Williams'
I wanted to write a poem
that you would understand
for what good is it to me
if you don't understand it
but you've got to try hard

*

you believed that God
wrote beautiful poetry
and Nature was his poem

certainly here in Tasmania
you could say he was
at his most Baroque
what with *Eucalyptus Regnans*
flame robins, blue wrens
wombats and the rest

you loved the flowers most
articulated them
for all to contemplate

consider *plate 5*'s
simple prayer
Blue Gum
and *Comesperma Volubile*
also known as *Love*

The Princess Theatre, Launceston,
18th October, 1995

What with the allusions I've been planting,
here's a fine coincidence! *The Tempest* on
in Launceston.

      (Mrs M launched out of Sydney
into storms; bolts of lightning shook the wings
when I took off from there).

      In the opening scene
sou'westers, heaving ropes, woofered winds
drowned the poetry and I slumped back in snootiness,
more so when Prospero like a terminal Gielgud led off
with fruity tremors and Miranda too zealously twitched
at every word; then Ms Ariel's see-through nipples
and tippy-toe walk! But when Ferdinand, bereft,
lamented the King his father's wrack, the play began
to move in every sense and when those lager-louts
Stephano and Trinculo bounced on it was uproarious circus
and I was *i' th' isle* for sure.

      (Mrs M adored theatre,
produced plays in Hobart. Remember *The Masques
of Christmas* in 1866? *Not with ivy garlands —|
Not with shadowy yew —| Not with holly berries|
Ruddiest of hue:| But with Summer's wealth of Roses
In the noontide of the year,| Ripe corn, sweet fruit
and posies| Crown we our Christmas here.)*

No tongue! all eyes! *Revels*, Mrs M.

Threads

1858: under what she thought
Wagnerian doom, the *curse of wandering,*

she was, at forty-six, prepared
to brave another change:

Twamley (with several more to come)
the latest humiliating move, the sixth

in fifteen years – miles back from the road
along a grinding track – she christened with

her Brummy maiden name, as I suspect,
to make a point about control, as if

sympathetic magic might
just stabilise their lives.

Cambria and *Riversdale*, alas,
each with their pretty gardens, now

hopelessly gone, the inheritance lost
with three out of her four boys

(sixteen, twelve, and nine) alive
(one a sickly child), both husband

(whose single asset was
a silver tongue) and wife at loggerheads.

*

1995: we dusted up the track on Prosser's Plains
to find the house. Two yapping dogs

ran figures-of-eight around the car. A young
woman fetched a grandad-gnome from hoeing

the vegetable patch to tell us how
a bolting horse had crippled him and how

at eighty-six he *took his time* and would *not*
pose for photographs. Had it not been

for eucalypts you'd have sworn it was an English Spring
along the Downs, so green the undulating fields.

Here in a rain forest at the back of beyond
Louisa Anne sent Charles to work at politics,

and here they told us things not found in print,
Charles's love of rum and of the sealing wax

(still there) she'd used to fix
spidery filaments across the cellar door.

Journal entry for Tuesday, 31st Oct.

Up at 7.30. Shower. Why haven't I thought of the cottage
as being like a sailing ship before? Inside's like cabins,
pannelled white. Heaviest load of washing yet! Wrote to
John. Out at half-past-ten in sun to post letters and stock
up at the supermarket. Met Louise (Andrew's Louise).
Then back again to read Patricia's *Wybalenna* before
popping into town for aerogrammes. Lunch at *Pierre's
(smoked salmon cornets)* when who walks in but Patricia
and a young-woman-with-problems (squirming to be out
of there, stiffening her face). Waldorf salad. P. likes the
poems about Louisa Anne, so does her psychiatrist
husband Eric. We talk of murders on the island. There's
been one recently. Girl on a beach. Went to Museum, saw
Kaye, photocopied the Grimshaw talk on Mrs M. Letter
from John, card from Michael. Back to the cottage,
finished *Wybalenna*, wrote to Bruce, then tried the
Flinders Island poem. Felt strangely weepy. Whisky last
night? Coming down to earth after the Grand Tour of the
island? M. in Berlin and on the phone about her mother?
First homesickness? Or realisation that the wind-up to
the residency's begun? Yes, all of these. Dimitris
phoned: come to Melbourne earlier! Day's simply disap-
peared. Time accelerating now. At 9.30 p.m. a drunken
Canadian knocks and asks directions to Bald Hill, can of
lager buckled in his fist. Wrote *Hobart* poem – and this –
in bed. Eleven o'clock.

Dangerous I know

but I'm beginning to think it – that
behind soft-hearted, generous men
there are usually restraining wives
quietly making things go right.

At least it seems so here among the ones
I've met, men still open to astonishments
and retailing them; women sardonic,
keeping things in check. From what

I've heard, Mrs M, it sounds the case
with you: Charles likely to be prodigal
and you earnest of success, even of success
for him. Where would Tasmania be

in the protection of mutton birds, black swans,
without your parlour insistences? the first
cable across Bass Straits? All this without
mention of your talents with the brush and pen.

A Poem for Wybalenna Chapel on Flinders Island

*In the working of the laws of God's
Providence, we have dispossessed
these poor people of this fair isle. In
that, we may hope, there is no sin;
but surely sin may lie heavily at our
doors, if we, blessed with civilisation
and Christianity, neglect to fulfil to
them the simplest duties laid upon us
by the requirements of Christian charity.*

The Rev. Thos. Reibey, August 1st, 1883

No sin, Mrs M? God help us! Your latter day
Augustines bouncing up and down
in creaking little cutters of 8 tons
shuffling from isle to far-flung Ozzie isle
transporting to the dispossessed
infernal bigotries, baptismal bounty,
beautiful services for the dead. Oh, yes,
they *read* to them about duty
and turning the other cheek, calling it charity . . .
left behind them *useful* tracts — absolving whom?

Let's cut the crap, my glib allusions
to Prospero and Caliban. Dispossession
was colonial savagery on a scale
that's even now too great to comprehend.

Would you really say there was no sin?

I'll quote you: *the very lowest creatures
in human form . . . a curiously close
resemblance to pug dogs . . . all the animal
instinct and adroitness for self-
preservation.*

All your bull about native
place names was really dilettante taste
for euphony ... like your lines about the sighing
breeze soughing *through mossy trees
'midst delicate maidenhair,* the rills
wimpling on round island rocks .../
By groves of fragrant sassafras.

How you giggled when dear Charles
did his impersonations of the dispossessed!

Family skeletons are being rattled here,
Louisa Anne, with a bad conscience
you'd call arrogant hindsight and some would
call their hardly bearable history.

Making an Exhibition

So that's what you think!

No chance for me to plead
rawness of the time,
uncompromising place —
the *scenery* that you applaud
from cars,

nor slovenly rum-glazed servants,
larders treacle-black with flies,
molestations of the elements,
feral bushrangers, fierceness
of the dispossessed?

                Be sure
your rightness isn't just display.
No time-and-place is ever
without guilts and shames.
We are all victims of something.

I've heard poets enjoy
parading self-righteousness
before like-minds.

I have my spies:
one of the two Mrs Merediths
who rsvp'd and attended
your reading in the Museum
was, dear Matt, no joke.

Louisa Anne Meredith four months before her death in 1895.

A Last Glimpse

Like crocheted yucca flowers
a lace bonnet froths
down over your shoulders.

In one light, periwigged,
Queen's Counsel at the Bench;
in another, like the Old Queen herself.

It's 1895, John Watt Beattie
is arranging you
in Hobart, your last months

tocking away. This time
the camera's not tilting up at you
to pursue elusive eyes:

it's looking down on a countenance
as laconic as a crotchety owl's,
on hands not flirting curls

but staunchly clasped against
the Day. You are beginning to think
it's not been worth the struggle,

writing to Parkes how you were born
or had put yourself under an evil star.
Perhaps you were thinking

of those Jane Austen days in Bath –
such a pretty and a little thing
daring in white muslin

to cross the Great Pump Room floor
and finger with a child's touch
that glittering thing on a blue ribbon

across the belly of the Duke of York,
causing vinegary old Queen Charlotte
almightily to smile.

Epilogue

Our revels now are ended.

Melbourne Central Cemetery

So finally you went
to Melbourne,
jostled across Bass Strait
aboard *The Pateena*.

*Presumptuous to count
on a return* you wrote
to grandson Jack.
And so it was. You died

at 171 Victoria Parade,
suburb of Fitzroy. At noon,
October twenty-first,
a century ago.

*

No hour-long flights,
no ship equipped
to take a body back
to Hobart. No-one

chipping *Beloved Wife*
on Charles's stone.
You're nowhere I
could wish for you,

like windswept Bruny Point,
the yellow orchids
below the lighthouse,
feet pointing to the snowy South,

or that stranded granite
Leviathan at Stanley, where
the night above the jetties
has such stars in it,

or Cradle Mountain
where people go to photograph
reflections in Dove Lake,
or then perhaps Green's Beach

among the frisky wallabies,
lumbering wombats, where dear Kaye
forgot the bread and almost set
on fire the picnic table, best of all

the walled, scented garden
of Albion House – books, pictures, music,
fine wines and food – that you (yes, you)
got me invited to.

*

Last chance, and something of
an off-chance, even if it bites the dust,
leaves ashes in the mouth, I mean
for me to pay respects.

Sunday, cemetery office shut,
no hope of documentary help,
map to show me your last bit
of colonising. Blow flies, blow flies

everywhere, nostrils, mouth. And so
I scuff cindery paths
round battered stones, hop
over rusted rails in Death's

neglected territory, the older
graves that say *This is the mark
we came to make.* But you
I cannot stumble on in time.

You're in here somewhere, not
talking, not anything. I head out past
new immigrant-Italian polished marble.
Who says Magnificence is dead?

Men, women down on knees,
washing, buffing dry, meticulous
with flowers, coddling their dead
as if just love might keep them near.

*

I tried my best. But time's a bully.
There are clouds to cut, Louisa Anne.

Select Bibliography

Notes and Sketches of New South Wales Mrs Charles Meredith. Penguin Colonial Facsimiles 1973

My Home in Tasmania, during a residence of nine years Mrs Charles Meredith. John Murray 1852

Tasmanian Friends and Foes, Feathered, Furred and Finned Louisa Anne Meredith. Marcus Ward and Co. 1880

The Penguin Anthology of Australian Women's Writing ed. Dale Spender. Penguin 1988

Louisa Anne Meredith – a Tigress in Exile Vivienne Rae-Ellis. Blubberhead Press 1979

The Story of Wybalenna Patricia Fitzgerald Ratcliff. The Glendessary Press 1975

Effects of Light – the Poetry of Tasmania ed. Vivian Smith and Margaret Scott. The Twelvetrees Publishing Co. 1985